What a Difference a Sloth Makes!

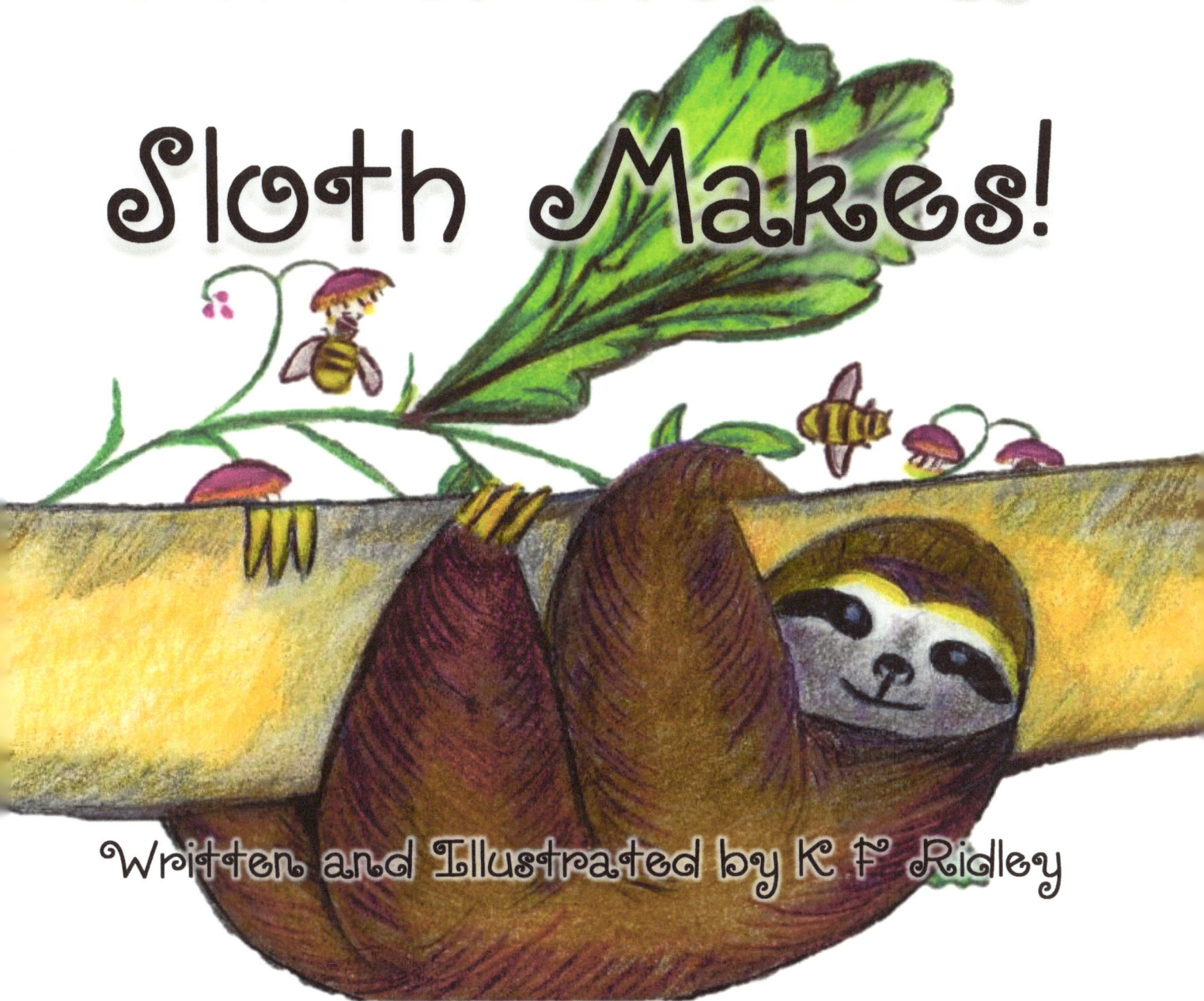

Written and Illustrated by K F Ridley

What a Difference a Sloth Makes!
All Rights Reserved.
Copyright © 2016 Kim F. Ridley
Written and illustrated by: Kim F. Ridley

Preschool-2nd, Reading Level – 2nd Grade

Summary: Although slow-moving and extremely quiet, a sloth discovers that it makes a great impact on the world we live in.

For information, address Little Roni Publishers
Children's Book Division,
submissionsLRP@gmail.com
www.LittleRoniPublishers.com

ISBN-13: 978-0692631195 (Also in eBook)
Little Roni Publishers / Byhalia, MS
www.littleronipublishers.com
@LittleRoniPublishers

Illustrations created by hand with colored graphite on paper.

FIRST EDITION

PUBLISHED IN THE UNITED STATES OF AMERICA

Dedication

To Jade, Livy, and Layla.

You make me smile.

What a Difference a Sloth Makes!

I sleep up
in a tree all day.

I guess I was
just made that way.

The birds fly high
and fill the sky.

They sing to you
a lullaby.

The bees, they buzz

from near

and far

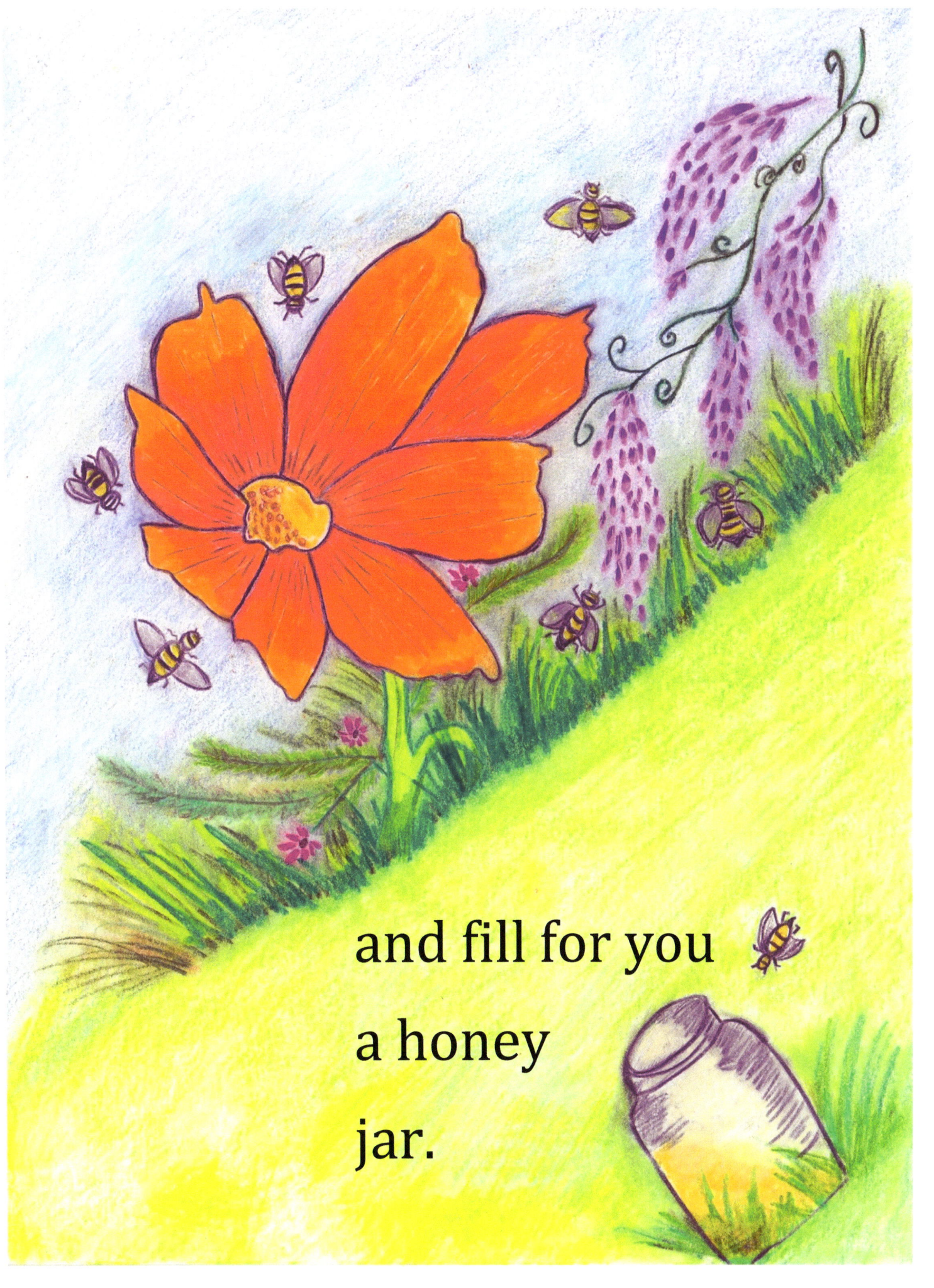

and fill for you
a honey
jar.

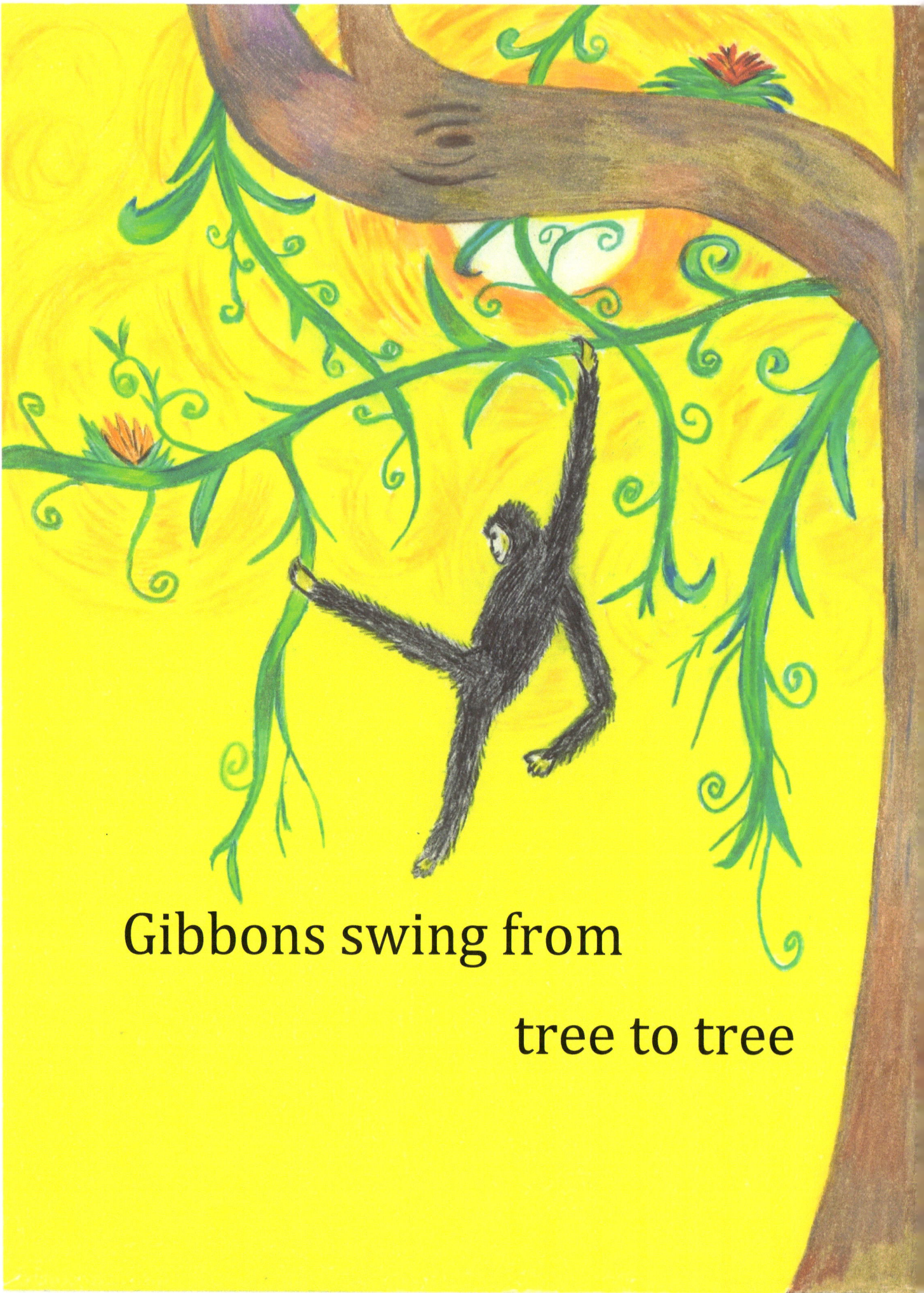

Gibbons swing from

tree to tree

leaping onto

vines so

joyfully.

The snake, he slithers
on the ground.

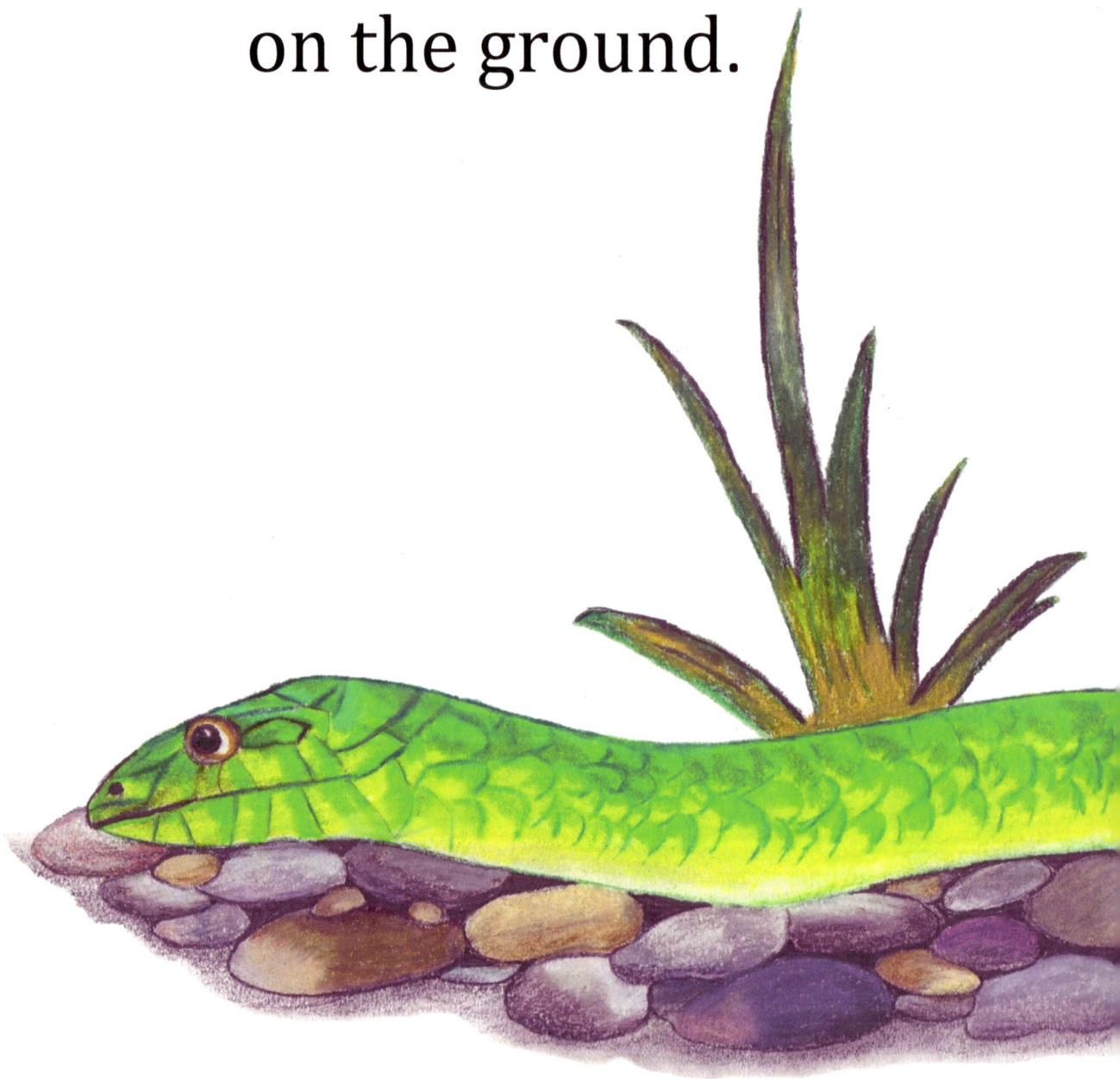

He's   L   O   N   G

and graceful

and makes no sound.

The leopard climbs in trees and spies.

He wears his spots

like many eyes.

Butterflies flutter with colors so bright.

Over a pool of water, they're a beautiful sight.

The elephant's trunk
swings and sways.

With water, he showers

as he sprays.

How can I

make a difference here,

up in a tree,

so filled with cheer?

I KNOW! I know what I can do
to make things brighter,
for me,
for
YOU!

I'll make our world
a better place.

I'll put a smile upon
my face.

Some Curious Sloth Facts

Some sloths have two claws and others have three.

About the Author
K F Ridley

As a child, KF Ridley was labeled as the kid with too much energy. Desperately, she did her best to conform to the ways of the world. Later, she realized she had to be herself. As a result, her imagination went wild.

These days, she funnels her energy, exuberance, and high-jinx into her writing and illustrating. There is no telling where her mind will take her—and you—next.

Kim lives with her family in Mississippi, with her two dogs, five chickens, and potbelly pig.

www.kfridley.com

Also by K F Ridley:

Middle-Grade
The Curse of Yama
The Castle of Family Secrets

Young Adult
Dirt

© LRP

More fun picture books from Little Roni Publishers

Henry's 'Magination (Reading Level-2^{nd Grade})
Collett Keel, (Illustrated by Ellen Sallas)
Does your imagination ever get you into trouble? Henry's sure does. His mother warns him not to make up stories, but surely nothing bad would happen just because he uses his imagination... Jump into Henry's 'magination and see where he takes you. Bring your imagination and add some fun of your own!
$14.54, 36 pages, full-color, softcover, ISBN: 978-1537065830
$4.99 Kindle

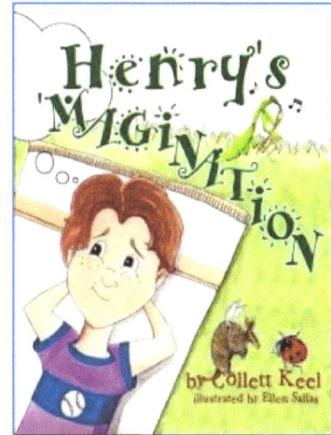

Harvey, Who's Good at Nothing, story and illustrations by Eric Eddy. Everyone around Harvey seems to be super talented. What in the world is Harvey good at? Delightful and creative tale, designed to look like a notebook which serves to encourage all young readers to create their own books while also increasing self-esteem. Ages 8-up, 36 pages, 8.5" x 11", 2015.

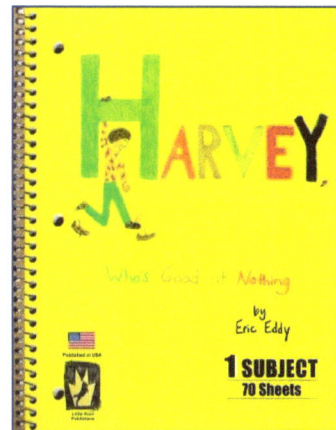

A is for Apple, a Horsey Alphabet, story and illustrations by Ellen C. Maze, with Elizabeth Little. Fun alliteration teaching the alphabet with the help of twenty-six super flexible and clever horse pals! All ages, 66 pages, 8"x 6", 2012.

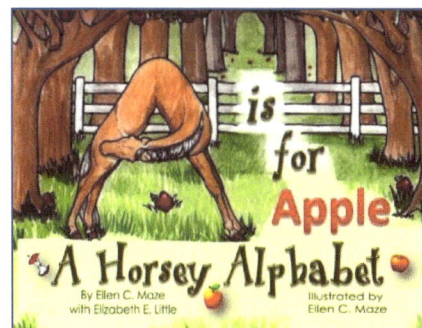

In Pursuit of Sir Unicorn, story and illustrations by Ellen C. Maze. What does the man do when his horse chooses a unicorn over him? It's a rhyming and epic adventure to get her back, and we all learn a lesson about friendship in the end. Ages 8-up, 46 pages, 8.5" x 11", 2013.

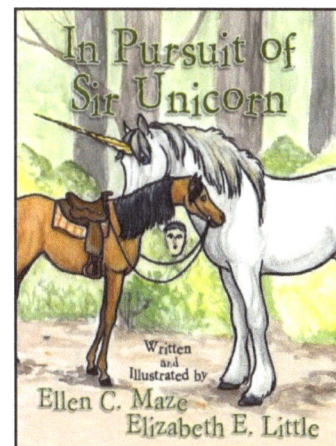

www.LittleRoniPublishers.com

LITTLE RONI
PUBLISHERS
Byhalia, MS

www.ingramcontent.com/pod-product-compliance
Lightning Source LLC
LaVergne TN
LVHW072055070426
835508LV00002B/108

*9 7 8 0 6 9 2 6 3 1 1 9 5 *